To Ca, Urs, Shea, Gar and Carm

TULLAMORE TRAIN

Neil Donnelly

ARLEN
HOUSE

Tullamore Train

is published in 2012 by
ARLEN HOUSE
42 Grange Abbey Road
Baldoyle
Dublin 13
Ireland
Phone/Fax: 353 86 8207617
Email: arlenhouse@gmail.com
arlenhouse.blogspot.com
www.arlenhouse.com

Distributed internationally by
SYRACUSE UNIVERSITY PRESS
621 Skytop Road, Suite 110
Syracuse, NY 13244–5290
Phone: 315–443–5534/Fax: 315–443–5545
Email: supress@syr.edu

978–1–85132–035–6, paperback

Typesetting ¦ Arlen House

CONTENTS

TULLAMORE TRAIN

A BLACK HORSE BROKE FREE

A black horse broke free from its grazing field,
a swarm of summer terrorist flies

sent it charging up the road, nostrils flaring,
head darting, until it saw an opening then

through the cornfield, sheaves rustling,
flanks gleaming, it turned into the high field

executing a perfect pirouette,
now a bobing black dot on the butter-coloured landscape

beyond which, unseen, the private housing estate
where the desperate housewives try

to placate their over carbohydrated children
while getting supper ready for homeward bound

husbands champing at the bit,
while the black horse in the far distance

motionless now, a regal
swan on a still evening lake.

UNCLES

Those strange tall men
who from time to time appeared,
then disappeared. The tallest with
the finger breaking handshake,
the small one who sang instead of talking,
the priest who when you held the gate
for him to drive away gave you a shilling
to get your hair cut. The well dressed one
whom your parents said was a *Playboy*,
him you rarely saw. The 'American'
with the cigar and the stare that first unnerved,
later you discovered a sea of kindness hid there
when he'd met you off the plane in New York
and gave you tips on how to make money,

and now you are an Uncle
to nieces and nephews
all freckles, curls and smiles,
the strange bearded man
who gets down on all fours
to act the goat. An uncle
who from time to time appears,
then disappears.

TULLAMORE TRAIN

Meeting the train
at Heuston
I'm looking for my mother
but no sign.
Perhaps she's fainted
and is lying in a carriage,
fear and foreboding
beaten down inside,
until there on the chequered
concourse standing puzzled,
wondering where I am,
relief and gladness
in me as I walk to her,
she smiles, *there you are, and I
thought you hadn't come.*

HENS ON SKYROS

The island's red hens are exhausted,
the cock is fit and frolicsome,
his boastful shrieks across the valley say
hey ho, hey ho, I've sent another on its way.

Hens' cower, scatter, a withered harem,
like builder and butcher he struts fine plumes,
he is indiscriminate, he shoots on pause,
he struts the wall, demands applause.

Those withered hens remind me
of Irish mothers in the fifties with that
shagged-out look, without much will,
before the advent of the pill.

NARROW LANE

Not friendly
at least not to me
a couple, two children and dogs,
as they walked down our narrow lane
to view their new house under construction

hammers against wood
pounding the clean spring air,
the clear spring air,
where the sky is all blue

then their house was finished
I never noticed them much
a year, eighteen months go by
'til on friday I see an ambulance

who's ill, I ask a neighbour, and am
told *all his lovely red hair is gone,*
totally bald, early forties.
The ambulance has just left
having brought him home to die

then a private lorry
came with stones to fill
the potholes; in a field
a car park sign went up,
farmyards were cleared,

not friendly
at least not to me
but now he's buried
he is mourned,

his journey,
like all our journey's,
where the road runs out
down a narrow lane.

IN THE OSPREY HOTEL

I'm sitting in the Osprey Hotel
and Dr Phil is on the giant TV screen
dolling out his endlessly practical American syrup.

My friend hates Dr Phil,
hates his shiny dome
his yard brush moustache
his calming voice
his prop forward strength
his gentle scolding
as he balms the self deprecators
the low self esteemers
the inadequate, the comfort eaters
the lonely deep depression suburbanites.

My friend will never admit
that when he was in hospital and Dr Phil
was beaming down at him from a wall bracket,
Dr Phil's American syrup balmed him.
My friend will never admit that *he'd* love Dr Phil
to come and sit and listen to his tale
hold his hand
pour some greeting card syrup in his ear
sooth him
sooth me
while I'm waiting in the Osprey Hotel.

THE KERRY DANCE

I was ten or so and I could sense it,
that unseen tug between a man and woman.

The piano new to the house
and my mother's suggestion to invite

Mrs Lawless in to play. While my
mother was in the kitchen making tea

Mrs Lawless's red finger nails in the front room
picked out the song and melody of

James Lynam Molloy's, 'The Kerry Dance',
and she and my father exchanged a smile.

A memory of sing-songs in Mrs Doody's
Boarding House near Kilbeggan Bridge

before my mother came to town,
before she and my father met.

Something passed between them,
something of another time.

BRIXTON STATION

Rail lines converge
beneath a bruised December sky

you are a frail sea shell
– twig hanging loose

in mounds of crisp snow
chill terror

words in throat chug
don't emerge

hands don't merge
like rail lines do.

Gurtymadden Suddenly

From Eyrecourt late one evening
rejoicing along a narrow country road,
suddenly a familiar road sign
where your Nantucket voice
once suggested there we meet.

You emerge
from the Atlantic Ocean bed
plunging me deep,
where are you?
what is your life now?

Almost twenty years,
no concrete news,
no answer
from passing
darkening trees.

PARTING

Your hand
extends determined
straight
freckles along the elbow

your head
bends determined
to the parting kiss
I'm not yet ready to give

between us
the wave
swells and swells
but does not break

inside the window
my youngest brother
holds you
tears so unexpected

what was it
you could not say
what is it
I didn't do?

suddenly you've destroyed
my hope in your strength,
it is too late now
the car moves away.

On the Steps of Basilique Sacre-Coeur

One of the hunting pack
of Arab young men sparrow flits
down beside a dark-haired girl.
You English? he says
the girl does not reply.
American, no? he persists.
Get lost!

He sparrow flits down a few steps
to the next girl
who gets his concentrated charm,
such ardour, chat up propulsion,
sheer intent

like young men
in the midlands
at carnival dances
or William Trevor's 'Bowser Egan'

on Ireland's motorways
or on the rat-runs home,
spunk driven, shooting
the load, unconsciously,
consciously
seeding for
immortality.

FEBRUARY

A pale Sunday afternoon sun stretches
across freshly ploughed fields

there are no phone calls
in or out, no Sunday papers.

In the garden
work to be done

four daffodils presented last night
January an anti-climax

next month it all begins.

SQUASHED ON A COUNTRY ROAD
for Cian and Leah

Saw him first when he was
a few months old, tiny
but for his big rust-red bushy tail
rolling on his back in the herb garden.
What a life to come, to forage in wind and hail!

Oh yes, despite the nightly
food I'd leave out he did away with rabbits,
some pheasants, the odd hen or two.
He drove me mad,
he was a fox, what else could he do?

We were used to each other,
I'd watch him eating, he didn't mind,
he'd bathe in the tub
then hang around
like a client in a member's club.

He was great value with visitors
out there in the sensor light, soaked
to the skin, his big rusty red tail limp
'Isn't he lovely', they'd say.
And he was. That once baby cub imp.

One night something was wrong,
sensor light didn't flood the back lawn.
I waited for him, no sign,
that fish previous night wasn't the best
his constitution hardly worse than mine?

Driving to town next morning
squashed on a country road
a dead fox, he knows these roads too well
couldn't be him, could it, paved with
good intentions, the endless road to hell.

GOOD FRIDAY

Skies grey as Christ's death day
chasing me from the room
stick behind
through the garden
into the field
purple lashes rise
on the back of the legs
running away

nowhere to run to
home is the only place

when all come back
from kissing the cross
apologise again
for that
or for the other
and Christ being dead
beg your forgiveness.

Parental Guidance – Explicit Lyrics

Why am I always curious
when I see such a sticker
on a CD cover and like
Adam in the garden tempted,
and when I read the lyrics
I'm bemused
at what *they* consider explicit,
always a let down
like Adam after the apple

scent of sulphur draws us

Joey Buttafucoo, who allegedly
had induced Amy Fisher to murder
his wife was sitting
opposite his father
at their office
desk eating a giant cheeseburger
when I sneaked a look in the window
of their Body Auto repair shop in Baldwin,
in the summer of 1993

scent of sulphur draws us.

REPRIEVE

Putting away your pictures
you have no strength
to zip close the carry folder

pictures from books
from head, heart, more power
since we parted

like skulls, bodies rocked
bone against bone
hearts torn asunder

dream to nightmare
belly deep down turning
feeling all the old

feelings I shouldn't
feel if I'm to go on
without you.

MERRYMOUNT HOSPICE

That man walking up
and down the corridor

yesterday,
is gone

in a box
like a bush fire

through his body spread
on Christmas Eve.

The Merrymount Hospice
a stone's throw from the Lee

is both a good and
a bad place to be.

CUL DE SAC

Our love is in a cul de sac
two steps forward, three steps back

in elegant dresses or states of undress
your beautiful face I long to caress

Sunday Mass, dressed to kill
sit all day on the windowsill

you plunge me in darkness
you bring me to light

you keep me on the straight and narrow
cut deep-down to the marrow

you so sweet and heaven sent
when you arrived all others went

a love at first I thought I did not need
became the love I could not live without indeed.

The callus on the hand that held the plough
the man, the plough, where are they now?

discarded like Xmas wrapping anyhow.

GALLERY CHANCE

In a little street with a big name
or was it a big street with a little name

let's just say in Scandinavia
I stopped at a gallery window

on the canvas inside a barge on a canal
straw blonde head appears and signals

her finger nail accidentally serrates
my palm when she hands me a catalogue

she has confused me with a buyer who is due,
she asks if I'd tag along as she has to pick up

her son at four. Once in the car he punches me on
the back of the neck, is this his customary greeting

or a reprimand to another momentary Dad?
He was getting his retaliation in first

I helped him with his homework
he allowed me that much

in her house by the river
he had calmed by bed time

she played some Ernest Raglan
she had met him once

why me? I asked
You were there, she said.

HANDS

Pass his grave
in the train

once he lived
he was here

I crawled over him
he cradled me

he covered my hands
five times

if I could
I'd unearth his resting place

and with my hands
cover his.

SPOLLENSTOWN

At a carnival once
a girl in a white wedding dress

we spent the whole day together
we were both about twelve

she said she knew I was going with
Dilly Dillane's sister and that we had a pact

whereby if we met in town we were not to
let on that we knew each other

never mind that we were 'going out'
and the strange thing is

that is something I *might* have *thought*
at that time because I was fearful

a belt from the crozier on one side
a belt from the parents on the other

who was that girl?
how did she know my thoughts?

OFFICE ROMANCE

It began as an office romance
well there was an awful lot of office
and little romance except
via her pigeon box and it didn't fly

she talked of Jurist Prudence
belief in Community
lack of a moral centre
the fall away of religious practice
but I said, *one day we'll return in triumph*
they'll throw palm beneath the Donkey's feet
and she knew I didn't mean it

used to wake up happy
with the thought of her
now I wake up grinding my teeth
with the thought of getting away

once she brought out the best in me
then the worst
somewhere in between was the rest of me
dying of thirst, dying of a long long thirst.

BERLIN APPLES

In the railway carriage
Turkish women gorge
on salami and fists of broccoli

my stomach rumbles
in a tunnel
I recall morning

at the market
stopped before apples
I couldn't buy

unlike all other times
I stopped beside you
buying them.

I SELDOM THINK OF YOU NOW

I seldom think of you now
except when I hear that Hoagy Carmichael song

or 'Rainy Night in Georgia',
my own words failed me then,

fail me now when I still can't find ways
to inscribe you, enshrine you, entwine you.

You originally from Thomas Hardy country
last saw your blonde head disappearing

round a red-bricked Nottingham corner
but that image too has faded

like the pale sun on an empty
Edward Hopper street – 'when soft rains fall and

I recall' or 'It's raining all over the world'
then you return, spring songbird,

yet I seldom think of you now.

Mirror

In the dream I'm in O'Connor Park,
Tullamore, at a football match,
then I'm taking in the countryside
at home prior to leaving

my mother busy with sudden chores
my father slows his shaving
journeys things loose about the room
I pack but can't fit everything

my father's footsteps on the landing
I compose a look for when
he'll come into the room
tears fall on the suitcase

I turn and put my head
in my father's arms
– *What's this!*
A strong man like you –

I am ashamed
this is the picture
my father will carry
after I've gone.

EL ESCORIAL

To the eight wonder
Felipe's *edificio*
squat-square symmetrical perfection
beyond the valley of the fallen

brandy coffee
your large brown eyes
past the straw sun on the plaza
to the snow topped mountains

Peckinpah would love it
transplanting the palace to Mexico
or Renais for another Marienbad
perfectly poised distance

like parents in womb time
you wear the navy blue jumper
bought the day of the unoriginal plot
hatched between Holborn and the Aldwych

an Angelus bell in the plaza
I'm at home waiting for my father
to give him the soccer results
you smile and at that moment

everything connects
thoughts of today ending are sacrilege
El Escorial pales to match
this fleeting perfection.

IN CADIZ

A lift in an empty hearse
from Seville and the sleeping black Guada
like a snake slinking away.
Lorry lights over dark february fields

illuminating small unripe oranges
then darkness again
in Cadiz in alleys
wet knives slink back in their leather beds

like black horses do in Lorca's verse
I seek out a pension and recall
fresh churros in Madrid last sunday morning
dipping into hot chocolate

till children spilling from mass
sent us to the *casa*
all day there till night
red dots in a navy blue dress

so quietly in the lift without a light
so quiet on the new pillow
stolen from your mother's house
so soft the stolen pillow

in wet alleys in Cadiz
arms of betrayed lost men
seek out night comfort here
the stranger running now

cursing out the pension sign
cursing out your soft brown eyes
a river that once flowed
towards me in the dark.

WEDDINGS AND FUNERALS

I love weddings, the woman in the taxi
on the way to the reception said

*I love when the dancing starts
do you like weddings?* she said to me

I prefer funerals, they are fixed, final
not laden with all that expectation,

all that guaranteed love,
weeds and some flowers will grow from a grave

and at the wedding
I'll vow to be your bloody-nosed eternal slave.

Day dirt from our clothes
night sweat from our sheets
her tears
my tears
everyone's tears who stayed and left

we piled you up
put the powder in
switched you on
you never complained
you gurgled
washed
spun and roared
until the final sputt sputt sputter
then silence

then the pause
in case you might start up again
but last night you faintly
sputt sputt sputtered
death-rattle-like
not an immediate stop
but a stop nonetheless

after twenty three years
you were graveyard silent
no paramedic's electric current
could revive you
you were finally
gone.

BRAMBLE

Becomes part
of the blood stream
the other's walk,
movement of feet, lips,
arms, and why wouldn't it
transfer, being in such proximity
such heat transferring,
melting iron
into liquid

sobering up
kicking the habit,
kicking to touch, climbing
back on the wagon, removing
splinters, away from each other
yet like every well meaning but faltering drunk
we fall from the bright clear blue sky
into the black bramble of night
we wish to be sober, to be clean
but we can't stand too much sobriety
or too much cleanliness.

FIN

Another blood speck
at your nostril
drone on of radio
dim light into blackness
slinging echo of the swish
round flying hands
other people
and their inadequacies
failing to out cancel mine.

In another room
sixth sense salmon turns her
train winding into darkness.

Whenever I'll see a long
golden hair on a black jumper
I'll remember
all the little lonelinesses
taken with you
on your road
from the sea
the road
without me.

My Father's Voice

Driving beyond Cloneygowen
I know we'll soon be home

but first the steep hill over the railway bridge
tension with St Mary's Church approaching

would I bless myself as we pass?
would my father stop talking to me if I didn't?

all of those moments that meant so much then
the church, its worship, might and power

now mean so little
while my father's voice means so much.

BRIGHTON

Green sea beyond silver railing
half-smile, windy street
rain spits, run back to the flat
and the two-bar electric

your blue eyes, shiny blonde hair
unspoken question
did you wash your hair for me
or did you just wash your hair

violin in the back room
a long tuneless tuning
then Vivaldi's 'Spring'
once there you look as though
you came to it by chance
and not to bring me to you

rummaging in the lanes
the old drunk dropping his cake
you helping him
his thanks in gripping your arm
my sudden jealousy
to have you back at our table

and later, unresolved calmness
walking to the green Southdown
sea so black
your eyes pinched tight
half-smile
Brighton fading.

TYBURN ORATORY
for Jan Farquharson

Just down from Marble Arch
on the Bayswater Road

site of 'The King's Gallows'
where the last Catholic martyr

Saint Oliver Plunkett
was hung, drawn, quartered in 1681

a young nun kneels facing the altar
she is motionless, calm, serene

outside the world whirls.

SINKING

First few days away, head down
concentrating on the task of being gone
letting go of all tantalisings, out of sight
not out of mind, boomerang back
comes spice herb garden, friday night
surprises, early morning rapture –
today wanted to text *sinking* to you
but fought it, keep wanting at bay
but you are there under the surface,
every second under the quicksand surface,
your back to the table at the moment I left.

THE HOUSE IN JAMESTOWN ROAD

Up to Dublin, for two westerns a day,
Theatre Royal then race to the Carlton,
at 5 my father collects me at Eason's,
my mind in Tucson, Arizona or some town
like Wichita Falls.

We stop at Mrs Sweeney's,
Jamestown Road, Inchicore
cups of tea, let the traffic pass before
the long long road to Tullamore.

Mrs Sweeney's eldest daughter
enters with a tray
swiz swiz of her stockings
loudest sound to my ear
her suspender clip strokes my thigh
as she slides in beside me on the settee,
oh, so near.

I forget Randolph Scott, Audie Murphy too,
hope they don't notice the change in me,
a fast munch on a ham sandwich
I stare hard at Harry Worth
on the black and white TV.

As the adults talk of Lynally, Mucklagh,
Rahan, an execution long ago
the Kirwin murder
that awful crime
and the secrets.

And what a great dancer Barney was
skilful, stylish, so full of charm
then after dances he'd hitch home

dancing shoes in brown paper
under one arm

Then the tension between him
and his brother Larry
no one knows why,
then despite a clemency petition
Barney waited four long months to die.

'2nd June 1943, they swung him'
Mrs Sweeney grinned and winked at me
Deirdre squeezed up from the sofa,
straightened her skirt,
topped up our cups with strong tan tea

In darkness we travelled home
my father and I
the long long road to Tullamore
Mrs Sweeney's daughter, the Kirwin brothers, that
    murder,
my head tumbling all that had gone before.

STRANRAER

Walking at night in Stranraer
or in any seaport town

brings me back to Wexford
the week I went Commercial Travelling

with my father, when I was eight
collecting English threepenny bits

to work the wall radio in the Talbot Hotel.

HURRYING TO ATHBOY

April, ushering a diminished summer
my mother's last minute
decision
to go thirty miles
to buy a new dress
in McElhinney's

we hurried against evening traffic
but got there late
she stared in darkened windows
walked back and forth,
then abruptly turned
into the Old Darnley for tea,

three weeks
after my father's sudden death,
hurrying to Athboy
to buy a new dress
intention is all.

LONDON IRISH TRIANGLE
(Archway, Camden, Kilburn)

On the street map at Archway Station
the 'Irish Centre' is clearly marked
but it no longer exists, abolished
by the Liberal Democrat Council
because most of the elderly
Archway Irish have sold up,
returned home and being back,
they hate it, it's not what they dreamed of,
and their pensions can't cope.

'I pity the poor Immigrant' Dylan sang
thirty years ago when unemployment
and fundamentalism
drove people out of Ireland
Archway, Camden, Kilburn pubs, full of
homesicks for the aul sod that failed them
or they felt they had failed it
dreaming of one day returning
to that Mayo coast road to build
a big house with a heap a kids

on Saturday nights
high strung fillies
colts and dolts
cantered then bolted
the Gresham, Forum and Galtymore
offered a temporary home
and like the boxer
in Paul Simon's song
'I took some comfort there'

'the Silver Cup Award Winner'
proclaims DeMarco's Café

had a bowl of their ice cream
once, same taste as Daly's
Harbour Street, Tullamore, in the fifties
when on the way back from the swimming pool
their ice cream took you to Italy
remember Tom and Eddie, town sophisticates,
back from Amalfi, browner than
cinnamon buns, declaring
'Italians girls look great from the back'

there's Madge Heron!
wild Donegal poet
worked as a skivvy
no Pushkin prize in her day

'World Cup, European Championships
All Ireland Finals!' on tarpaulin at a Kilburn pub
Arab, West Indian, Indian,
Nigerian stall holders
pavements cluttered
thirty years ago the Grange was a cinema
it is now the Victory Christian Church
fundamentalism back again.

BUNDORAN

Tousled brown haired
girl waiting to cross
at College Green

scent of sun cream

red and yellow boat
coming from the sea to sand
and our mother rubbing in
the balm of Nivea.

EXQUISITE PAIN

Have I met you in some former life?
Are you some unknown half-sister?

or is it simply your girlish beauty
that causes such exquisite pain

blue sky beyond bare branches
a distant shore

breaking my own rules
crossing and re-crossing the border

tease, laugh, talk, with winter approaching
love is a warm coat

in the quiet moments
when you are gone

you return
in space between.

SWEET CACOPHONOUS DIN

On the railway platform
a woman pushes a buggy

we did not take that adventure
we might have had a girl

who despite her father's nose
her mother's knotty curls and dimpled chin

a true beauty who danced and sang
and made a sweet cacophonous din.

INTIMACY

Men look forward
to driving
alone,
football matches
rounds of golf
building sheds
ways to escape
that awful stultifying
stupefying,
chest-choking intimacy
which most of us crave
yet need to flee from.

AUSTRALIA

I came back in a fog
blasted the stereo way up

all the calls to the Samaritans
tonight came from me

you are going to Australia
what the hell's with Australia

that isn't with me!

KENMARE PIER, NIGHT

Cannot see water
only a stone's plop
makes me know it's there

thick blackness spreads
so soothing this embalming
liquid of night

through the black expanse
a car's headlights
on the steel grey bridge

if that were my father's car
going quietly home,
how perfect.

LOVE BOMB

He had glasses
his black hair had a recent spiky cut
he looked happy
he had a small travel knapsack
and a white plastic bag from which he took
sweets and a mobile phone
he offered me a stick of chewing gum
I declined,
thanked him and asked where he was going
Stafford, he said, then realising he had just come from there
Crewe, I mean, Crewe, I've just spent the weekend with my Dad,
he smiled a big smile
And now you're going home.
Yes, he said, *I'm going home to Mum.*
He had spent the weekend with his father who had
love bombed him.

His mother would meet him at Crewe,
take him home,
love bomb him all over again
then it would ease off,
the love bombing; ease off then almost
disappear until
the next visit to Stafford and those intense
few days there
then back up again to Crewe.

When people are first attracted
the early days are marked with intense phone,
text, and floral bombardment
love bombing smoothes over potential fault lines
each fault line is polyfillered over
with forty-eight hour intense
carpet bombing. Then a child,

who in turn in the early days
is intensely love bombed.

Flowers we don't water
wither on the ledge.

All the time when we were growing up
and we shared a room with a sibling and each of us
longed for a room of our own
and then in a matter of years
we are expected to share a room,
for the rest of our lives,
with someone who is in essence
a complete stranger.

The train slowed
coming into Crewe.
the boy stood up.
Goodbye, he said
Mind yourself.
I will, he grinned
he walked down the carriage
and joined the others who were leaving.

ARDEN VISIT

House I was sometimes fearful,
sometimes happy

my mother in the kitchen,
in the garden

in the bathroom
the old bath we all washed in

smell her Coty hair oil
her auburn hair glistening

visit her grave
where so many times we went

to place flowers on my father's
too soon place of rest

neither are in the earth
they are skipping and dancing in the street.

JOE DOLAN ON THE UNTER DEN LINDEN

In Berlin, a text from a midland friend
Joe Dolan passed away today

going to a Joe show
meant you didn't go home alone

home alone in winter is never
the answer to anything

past the palace of the Prussian monarchs
down the boulevard of Linden trees

towards the Brandenburg Gate
on the 26th of December 2007

in a light brown suit and Cuban heels
I saw Joe Dolan saunter,

that marquee in Kearney's field
afterwards in the back of her Morris Minor

the farmer's son couldn't get the nurse's bra strap
undone until she undid it for him

she was escaping casualties and the terminally ill
he was escaping everything else

in Greece once, a Spanish girl asked
*who is that powerful voice coming through the street
loudspeaker?*

An Irish singer, came the reply
and that man was momentarily closer to her
Andalusian smile.

IN A FAMILY GATHERING

In a family gathering
mention of your name

then on to another story
but in me with that mention

all time stops still

where did you go?
Where is the memory of you?

Once you were amongst us
life and soul

some of your sayings
linger in the ether

since you dropped
out of the living world.

DEFYING TIME

It is your birthday,
every year it is a good day.

I remember the Mitchelstown
stop off; unwind, freshen up,
pot of tea, calm down
before the endless,
endless road ...
warning sign markesman
soldiers on manouver
training for Bosnia, Kosovo,
Africa or Lebanon.

Into Fermoy
over the Blackwater
right at the T Junction,
then on out to the first traffic lights
red stops me,
you race across in front
late for a lecture,
exam in two week's time,
you said when you got in the car;
on that lift into Cork city
twenty seven years ago,
defying time.

It is your birthday
every year it is a good day.

RESOLUTE SEPTEMBER

We climb the gate into the field
shoal of blackberries on the wet hedge

hen pheasants take flight over crew-cut cornfield
rabbits run for cover

at least the foxes and the shooters
didn't get them all

there will be another spring
this is a resolute september.

WALKING IN PARKS

It felt so good to walk with you
even though our time was short

once we were lovers
now we live oceans apart

all the years we'd been together
in stormy hail and tranquil heather

and now like elder couples do
we walk in parks and regret how time flew

in between the pruned rose flower beds
You tell me of your future plans

how often have I heard that how and why
walking in parks is full of plans that go array.

TULLAMORE STATION
after 'Adlestrop' by Edward Thomas

Yes, I remember Tullamore Station
because for a time I worked there
as a summer relief clerk
tracking goods mislaid somewhere.

Passengers from Dublin alighted
taxis spirited away stragglers who lingered
magazine bundles from Eason's on the trolley waited
schoolboys' light fingered.

In the waiting room once
a young eloping couple were apprehended
we staff were asked to keep hush hush
least said, soonest mended.

September and the last time
I cycled home, no blackbird anywhere,
Charleville and Rahan fields behind
had been well treated, I was happy there.

RETURNING

I open the door
my father is standing outside
Won't you come in?
he looks up towards the roof.

The house he built
once his home.
Come on in
see what transformations have been made
grandchildren playing in the hallway.

He doesn't move
he looks across the road to the hospital
how could he do that to us
not come in
not curious to see how we are getting on.

I ring the doorbell
it brings my mother cautiously along.
Da's here
she looks puzzled,
What do you mean? she says.

Looking at me, looking past me
Da might like to look through the house,
There's no-one there,
she doesn't believe me
thinks I'm crazy.

Alright so
he's living in another town,
living another life,
living with a whole
other different family

I often have that dream
now my mother too is gone
yet she and he are
constant ghosts
returning.